THE TOCK BOOK
Poetry for the Last Days

Ira Mae Lewis

VANTAGE PRESS
New York / Washington / Atlanta
Los Angeles / Chicago

To My Children

FIRST EDITION

Published by Vantage Press, Inc.
516 West 34th Street, New York, New York 10001

Manufactured in the United States of America
ISBN: 0-533-05908-9

Contents

The Tock Book

The Man We Must Marry

I talked with my mother,
And she had said,
"Daughter, marry the right brother
Or better not wed."
But who is the right brother?
My head it does ponder,
A smile, a tear,
A man "over yonder."
Full of cheer and all smiles,
Is my aunt named Ann?
She knows whom to flee,
But will catch as she can;
If you wish to know why,
It's cause "Fred's on parole."
I wonder but how she continues so bold.
So I summated, concluded,
Withheld, and withdrew;
A jailbird's no husband.
I think then she knew.
The conclusion was mine,
Bought, sealed, and collected,
The man whom I married
She must have rejected.

The Shredded Ghost

You sleep as if you were not there,
As if you would not, could not care,
As if you were then called away,
To fly, pursue a place to stay.
If clouds must burst and fall apart,
Would you but dupe the Master's art?
Why keep your heart away from me,
While in the willowed dust there be?
Dear maidens lost they call the "not,"
The bloomers everyone forgot.
Whoy do you shake your wretched sleep
While in the night's pit now I weep?
I'll go there too one somber day,
There to remain, return to clay,
To hope a spirit in me dwell,
Which saves a soul from burning Hell.

The Looming Car

In my bleak, go car
I'll soon be back
Not to go far
And even thought the
 Hulk I be
I'll toss this car into the sea. . . .

I'll swish and whack
And ride this sack
And wish with something
 new to cope
I've tumbled and tossed
 in this mad ride
And cast away my every hope. . . .

And though I wish some
 way to ride
Someday somehow to
 climb this hill
The seams of life have
 burst inside
And called upon my every will.

Extravaganza

I almost served the other day.
Whom shall I blame or venerate?
But then I caught myself some way.
There was no time to hesitate.
Foil and toil, the countless days
  of little rest
Incessant rage, I've worked and tried.
  I've done my best.
The little children, they knew not
How Santa Claus went out and got.
Pray let them play, the Rascals, too
As each day goes, they start anew.

To the Crank Caller

I see you as a brother
Who runs around to "be,"
The future all a-scatter,
The pirate's wretched sea.
The night was really lonely.
You called me all there through.
Instead of going to Mother,
I think I'll come to you.
The day has come again.
Suppose you've gone to sleep.
Tonight you'll call again
Or will you go "beep, beep?"

The Centrum Speaks

If I were you,
I'd rise and face the morning dew.
I'd meet the glowing sun, then get
To work and later learn to fret.
I'd let my work be done, but good,
And learn to try as others would.
For good can overcome that lust.
I'd wait the time of day till dust,
And fear but really would not run.
I'd think by night my work was done.
The stars and countless overcast
  I would not mind,
Nor trust the past.
I'd go, and then I'd go some more,
Until I'd reached the end, that door
That locks but leads to other roads,
Which go and gather other loads.

The Goofy Girl

I goofed a lot.
I goofed my spill
To find a universe at will.
I goofed some more
And told on you;
How could they know
I'm goofy, too?
And who's to help
My goofy cause,
The road to pluck
And real applause.
If you were me
And I were you,
Would you be good
And goofy, too?

The Skeptic

Time is now, and time is dreary.
Fleeting moments come anew.
Time is place, and place is placement,
And I know not what to do.
Though at first I'd get a show boat,
Get a rocket ship, canoe,
But the wax got in the Glocoat.
Slippery sliding we went through.
And if you're tired and also weary,
Never tell your life you're dreary,
Seeking for a plague anew,
Never tell your life you're through,
For you're going to find another place,
Where night and dreams shall meet.
Wear your thoughts but clear, my brother.
Wear them; let them guide your feet.

The Countess

The gardener said
To the girl in red,
"Go get Miss Molly Clause.
She prances in her room all day
And never claims a pause.
She thinks that bearded men will guide her
And with their thorny fangs beguile her.
They too shall prance around the room
And never seek or bid a doom."

Man's Faith

The winding faith in man creates
A perfect split in all his gaits.
If he can overcome the spin,
Which he has whirled, without, within.
Straight ahead the road is just;
A winding one to win he must.
Don't forget the looking back.
You've done it,
Oh! My, what a whack!

The Courtly Ride

The king was sad yet singing;
He knew he had his love.
The town church bell kept ringing,
The last call to the dove.
"So I see," spoke he,
"You ride in rhythm.
Quiet maid, I deemed you were.
You miss me, Dear?
Well, I'm right here
Climb in and call me sir."
"I don't care," cried the maiden.
"My name is Mrs. Wertz."
The king was sad.
He was so mad.
He thought the queen was certz.

The Daily Tides

There they go again,
The sealess, sensual race;
None too strong, and yet
All seek the same sure pace.
Who really ever knows
What endless gauge afloats?
The world is full of gore;
'tis waste
To run so wildly and gloat.

The Crisis

She was a Chasa Wasa child, Kibitz,
And she knew she had to play the Ritz,
But she ran too far
To find her way out tha
With a man who jollied in his fits. . . .

Chorus

Do you believe it? Yes.
Do you believe it? No,
Hey, man, please tell
Which way to go. . . .

She dashed a bucket, cool and coze
From his head down to his toes
While on his cozy couch he lay
On his "high bed" made of hay. . . .

Chorus

She ran away down to the beach
To find a lesson she could teach.
The sharks, barracuda, gave her a whirl.
At least she thought it in her world. . . .

Chorus

She ran back to her home
From whence she thought she'd never roam.
He taught her a lesson with his tongue-lash skill
And vowed if she wet him
He was sure to. . . . Spill.

Chorus

So you see about Sally Ann
Who went around playing in sand.
We can tell what she
Wanted on a cloudy day,
Cause she lost what she
Counted when she ran to play.

Chorus

The Plague

Dear Lord, I thought that I had learned,
But your universe is so vast
And your ways are so profound
That I have nothing but to yearn.
Pray, let me do the right thing, Lord,
When pledged to thee.
I must look back in pain and see the gourd
From whence I licked the dust.
For true it is, there is guile in me;
Who deemed the sacred sword?
Who must indeed this botherer be?
Indeed it is the Lord.

Somnambulism

If dreams come true,
Why should I not remember you?
I fell asleep the other day
While you were wide awake at play.
I dreamed I lost you to a clown,
Who turned you round, and round, and round,
And tossed you up into the air,
And told you that he did not care.
When all my dreams failed me at once,
I dreamed I lost you to a dunce,
Who sat upon a wooden stool,
In a corner, in the school,
And told the teacher he knew naught,
Forget the candy treats she bought.
He bounced and bounced upon the stool,
And started once to scream out, "Fool,"
And as he bounced he turned away,
Then ran out through the gate to play.
Feigning well, I would not know
Which way my stupid dreams would go.

The Little One

I am indeed so very small,
I'd like to make a wish I'm tall.
Were I to praise you for your anguish,
This would afford me some liberty;
Were I to tolerate your malcontent,
This would afford me some virtue;
Were I to give you a helping hand,
This would afford me some virtue,
Were I to aid you in your search,
This would give sublimity;
Were I to seek you with your push,
This would indeed give me luck.
Forgive me for wishing,
For I am but a child.

Personality

Personality is a thing of doubt,
Which one cannot live without;
We vegetate and live in waste,
Then weather through a dying pace.
The thought and aftermath we search,
As birds do twig-hunt on a birch,
And when we have, we know not how,
And when we don't, we then must plough.
We keep the pace and run too far,
Forget the race, leave doors ajar.
But still in spite of how we sit,
We hope the personality won't split.

The Children Grow

Oh! My dear, you have come at last.
Eureka, you have journeyed far,
Amidst folks, cities, and the past,
Your ways and wisdom now bizarre.
Your wonders, like all, were cast,
Upon life's rivers, into the sea;
The dreams you had are now the past.
It's true your life must really be.
And now that you do know the pace,
May I but ask if it's too late
For you to walk life's laureate haste,
Know when to stop and when to wait?

The Gamemaker

He makes and takes and splits the air;
While in a spin he does not care.
His record has run off the reel;
He tries to hide but not to kneel.
He wants to make and take some dough.
The Big Wheel's fares he must not show.
He seeks to go another way
To stake his claim and somehow play.
Another wheel turn now he'll take;
Another wheel turn now he'll make.
So finally he gets to play,
The "Big Wheel's" game, which makes his day.
The payoff 's tops, and he can win.
His universe begins to spin.
He took his lot and won the game
And later at the door lay lame.

The Quaking Man

When souls burst out and spirits mate
Man does not really hesitate,
Expecting well his worth in gold,
And waits to see the time unfold.
Concluding on his very soul, the
  burst of time,
That which we sought when we were blind,
The fair we thought would never end,
And yet that time will burst again
And, too, will burst the loading tears
To give us life a million years.
O blinking time, why cast thy spell?
The peace God makes
No one can tell.

Nonsense

I say there, "Mr. Happiness,
Where did you get your spoon?
I'd like to learn about your source,
As well as Mr. Moon."
"I have no source," cried Happiness.
"Am just here for a while.
But should you keep in touch with me,
I'll lend a little smile."
"The lady with the printed dress
Has visited with me,
And brought out Mr. Happiness.
This is no crime, you see.
And whether she wears pocket dress,
Or one with padded yoke,
There are as many on the moon,
As there are laughing folks."

Do What You Wanta

Don't get caught on the raft.
Don't sign up less you really have to.
And do what you wanta do.

Chorus

Do what you wanta do.
Times are bad.
Don't be a softie over thing you had.
When you believe it's a useless day,
Do what you wanta and stay, stay, stay.

Don't hang it up, high out there.
Keep your feet on the ground
Cause, really, I care.

Chorus

Don't eat up all the good food,
Cause moderation is very good.
There's plenty all over the U.S.A.,
So do what you wanta
And stay, stay, stay.

Chorus

Don't slay people all over the place.
Drugs are not good; they generate waste.
There are times for all things. Don't gloat
gloat, gloat
And don't bother with drugs, cause that's dope,
dope, dope.

Chorus

A Dream

The temporal dominion of Man
Gives thanks to God, the Mighty Hand
Who lets us breathe and live and grow,
Directs our paths in which we go,
For I have dreamed and understood. . . .

I wish to live and try to row
My boat of life, so it will glow.
The things to give breath to the soul
Which supplement, direct, control. . . .

And when I am down and out of steam
A ray of light gives me a gleam.
I gaze into the sky and see
A shooting star where Heavens be. . . .

Hear cold and roaring winds outside
Wherein the doors of warmth I hide,
Then wait and see the rising sun,
Hear soothing rain that's just begun. . . .

This is to me, really, a dream,
And other phases merely seem
Through roads of life I shall now go
And hope my seemly beams will glow. . . .

The Cry of Youth

I'm in this group
Therefore in the soup,
For me the man does sway.
I'll find a better way. . . .

Evidence increases.
The heart of brother ceases,
Dancing on the parquet floor,
Watching who comes to the door. . . .

My way was mighty fine
Until I went too far.
When I but broke the line
I wished for my guitar. . . .

My voice, I sing; it's sweet,
The music I do make
Who told the law mankind
That new car I did take?

He ran me through a loop.
When? I forgot to say,
So now I wish the group
Or any old school day. . . .

The group took me too fast,
A hop, a skip, in time.
Into the street it cast,
Back to the old soup line. . . .

In line I learned to stop
And have a fast, filled day
Around the corner clock,
The fastest way to play. . . .

They book you, yes, the most
And put you on the grill
The grill was hot, the toast,
The page lines he did fill. . . .

While in the old lock-up
I thought about the days
When I was in the school,
The end of summer's haze.

Every Day Is Saturday

I wash the clothes and boil the rags
And tip the toes and toe the tags,
Stay good and whole and tried and true
And work and scrub the whole day through.

The evening brings the newsman, though.
I rest and listen to him glow.
He tells of all the day's events
And sells his wares and gives his hints.

I sew awhile and drink some tea.
The coffee hour was half-past three.
And when it's time to go to bed,
I hope that nothing vile I've said.

Because, you see, the day grows old.
Memories of yesterday unfold.
I saw the mail this tried, true day
And listened to a child at play.

So now, you see, it's time to sleep,
Get up tomorrow, sow and reap.
Repeat the cycle then again.
Get up; try not to show your hand.